I0884673

SENIOR ADULT
Program Builder
No. 3

Resources for fellowship, inspiration, and outreach

Compiled by Paul M. Miller

Lillenas Publishing Company
Kansas City, MO 64141

Contents

Poems for Recitation

Readings, Sketches, and Service Helps

A One-Act Play

POEMS FOR RECITATION

Time

Every tick and tock of the cosmic clock
  Measures time that we have spent;
All the days and years, with their laughs and tears—
  How I wonder where they went!

How the time has flown! All the joys I've known
  Seem as only yesterday;
And the grief I've borne, when my heart was torn,
  Helped illuminate the way.

As the time goes by, I have wondered why
  I must always forge ahead.
I would like to stay in a bygone day,
  With the kind words someone said.

But the clock ticks on—with tomorrow's dawn,
  New adventures are in store;
And today will be only history—
  We can't live it anymore.

By celestial laws, we can only pause
  To reflect upon the past.
But we'll soon be free, in eternity,
  Where the clock will stop at last.

—Vernon R. Harris

The Eternal Lifeline

Lord, give me the faith of the spider
  To trust the invisible lifeline
For I know it is there, always waiting.
  One just for me, all mine.

Help me to hang on in trouble,
  To trust when the going is tough;
To climb up the highest of mountains,
  No matter how high or how rough.

Lord, You are my invisible Lifeline,
  I give thanks that You are there;
Thanks for Your eternal guidance
  And the lifeline that I call prayer.

"They trusted, and thou didst
  deliver them" (Psalm 22:4).

—Helen Kitchell Evans

A Gift from God

Another grandchild, so tiny and
    sweet,
A gift from God—a special treat;
Another grandchild to hold and
    love,
A gift from God in heaven above,
Another grandchild to pray over
    and train
By our example, for God's way is
    very plain,
Another grandchild with which to
    play and grow;
A gift from God—we surely do
    know!

—Wanda E. Brunstetter

Satan's Still the Devil

Old Satan loves to blind the human mind,
So that the path of life we cannot find.
He loves to make us think that all is well;
Although, if lost, we're on our way to hell.

He told dear Eve, the world's first lady, "God
deceives you, child; He rules you with His rod!
He wants to keep you in the dark—a fool!
You cannot find yourself beneath His rule!

"The fruit that God forbade you eat," he said,
"Contains the key to brighten up your head!"
"Of course," Eve said, "I see! The fruit is good!
It's food for thought! I'll share the news! I should!"

Old Satan's still the same today—a fiend!
He likes to make us think that he's our friend.
Then, having tasted his forbidden fruit,
We learn too late we are his new recruit!

—David Olds

Morning

Turn first to God in the morning.
Turn to Him in prayer;
Tap the inner source of strength,
You'll find abundance there.

Ask and you will receive.
Christ's Spirit frees us from fear;
Renewed confidence quiets anxiety
When our Lord is very near.

Be assured of the right guidance,
For God's way is always right;
His calm and trusting Spirit
Gives us strength for each day's
flight.

"The eternal God is thy refuge, and
underneath are the everlasting
arms" (Deuteronomy 33:27).

—Helen Kitchell Evans

Coping

Feeling touchy one spring
morning—
In a huff I stamped outside;
For a time I walked all by myself,
Then God was by my side.

When I returned, I was at peace;
Now, regardless of the weather,
When I feel down, I walk—with God
Till I get it all together.

—Florence Boutwell

God Is So Busy

God is so busy; He has much to do;
But He's always there, loving me and
you.

He cares for the world from sky to
sea,
But He cares most of all for you and
me.

God keeps the sun all bright and
warm;
He sends a rainbow after the storm.

He keeps the ocean wet and blue
And covers my yard with morning
dew.

God cares for the world from sky to
sea,
But He cares most of all for you and
me.

He makes the raindrops and lets
them fall;
He keeps the trees all growing tall.

He keeps the sand along the shore;
God does all this, and so much more.

He keeps the snow all cold and white
And all the stars twinkling at night.

He holds the clouds up in the sky
And keeps the birds all flying high.

God is so busy; He has much to do,
But He's always there, loving me and
you.

God cares for the world from sky to
sea,
But He cares most of all for you and
me.

God plans for warm days when
flowers grow
And wintertime when He sends the
snow.

He makes a morning to start every
day
And hears me at night when I kneel
to pray.

He puts smiles on friends' faces to
make us glad
And makes loving arms for when we
are sad.

God is so busy; He has much to do,
But He's always there, loving me
and you.

He cares for the world from sky to
sea,
But He cares most of all for you and
me.

God gives the flowers their colors
and smells
And plans for turtles to carry their
shells.

He plans for fish to swim in the
seas
And for birds to build their nests in
trees.

He plans for kittens to purr and
meow
And for puppies and dogs to bark
and growl.

Only God can do all that, we see,
And only God cares so much for me.

God is so busy; He has much to do,
And always He's there, loving me
and you.

—*E. Elaine Watson*

Trivial Poorsuit

A man walked briskly down the
street;
Most faces he passed were grim.
He started smiling, tipped his hat,
And people smiled back at him.

His poor suit was grayed and
shabby
But his smile, sincere and bright.
To him, his clothes were trivial.
People's smiles were pure delight.

—Lillian Pittman

October: God's Handiwork

October,
The loveliest month,

Advances:
Slowly matures.

A mood
Of festive,
Seasonal colors
Lingers.

Moving leaves
Of burnt gold,
Deep crimson
Brighten the maples,
Stir:
Continue autumn's promise
In such frosty air!

—William Beyer

Retirement

Retirement is an agonizing choice.
So many decisions to make.
Should I move or stay put forever?
I just don't dare pursue a
mistake.

Should I give up my lifework? Sell
my home?
These thoughts hound me, day
after day.
I am so frustrated . . . can't sleep at
night.
Guess I'll stay where I am . . . I'm
OK.

—Lillian L. Pittman

Growing in Grace

Today I'm growing in majestic grace,
But what a total waste I was before
I stepped across the threshold of the
Door
To sit with Jesus Christ, to take my
place.

No longer does my tortured soul
complain
That life is vanity of vanities,
That life is very long and filled with
pain,
That life's a series of futilities.

Today old things are old and I am new.
My soul at last has found tranquillity.
The knell is now a joyous symphony.
Praise God! I'm on a gold avenue!

Oh, won't you taste and see the Lord
is good?
He wants to be the anchor of your
soul.
Oh, won't you step inside His
brotherhood?
He wants your life to be in His
control.

—David Olds

Within the Heart

Senility not ability?
Not true! Not true! Not true!
Think of all the great things
That older people do.

Grandma Moses wasn't an artist
  Until advanced in age,
So don't underestimate us
  And place us in a cage.

We have the benefit of wisdom,
  Of all our days of living;
We have learned that in life
  We need to be forgiving.

We have all contributed
  Skills to society,
Helped set life's standards
  With great propriety.

Sure, we have arthritic pain—
  Every day we live
But we keep on going
  And we have much to give.

We may look as old as Moses
  But we don't act the part,
For we have youth and gladness
  Sealed within the heart.

—Helen Kitchell Evans

To a Nurse in the Nursing Home

What are you thinking of, Nurse,
  When you stand looking at me?
Just a crabby old woman
  Who will soon be 93?

You say that I get all mixed up . . .
  Can't remember anything . . .
Forget where I left my glasses,
  My purse, and my wedding ring.

I'm always losing my sweater . . .
  I'm always spilling my soup . . .
But listen, once I was young as you,
  Not always a nincompoop!

True, my carcass is crumbling . . .
  Hearing's bad; I cannot see . . .
But take a good look . . . I'm a person!
  Take a close look . . . It's me!

—Lillian Pittman

I've Heard His Voice

The presence of God helps me to
    see,
To appreciate all that's been given
    to me;
To welcome the future I face today,
To live for now in God's true way.
I feel surrounded by His loving
    grace;
I feel ready to work in my special
    place;
With His guidance and power with
    Him I rejoice
I am truly blessed, for I've heard
    His voice.

"We give thee thanks, O Lord God Almighty, which art, and wast, and art to come" (Revelation 11:17).

—Helen Kitchell Evans

God Cares

It might seem like no one cares,
But God does.
It might seem like no one hears,
But God does.
It might seem like no one
understands,
But God does.
It might seem like no one's real,
But God is.
It might seem like hearts are
callous,
But God's isn't.
It might seem like hurts can't heal,
But they can.
God told me so in His word
[Malachi 4:2].

—Marjorie Taylor

Angels

When we are ill and depressed
We are often given much love;
Cards, phone calls, and letters
Are like "messengers of God" from
above.

They bring us the needed comfort
To help us through the day;
They give us the strength and
support
For which we so often pray.

Friends and sometimes strangers
Are the instruments of God's care;
We are entertaining angels
Though we may be unaware.

"Be not forgetful to entertain
strangers: for thereby some have
entertained angels unawares"
(Hebrews 13:2).

—Helen Kitchell Evans

A Senior's Prayer

Lord, I sit today in my rocker.
It's about all I can do.
You know that I'm old and crippled
And my abilities are few.

But I pray for a child who's hurting.
Her mother is hurting too—
For that's the way that mothers are.
You can ease their pain. Please do.

There's a teen who's having problems
With his parents and at school.
I ask You, God, to help him
Think about the Golden Rule.

A man has mired himself in sin.
His life is full of pain.
Remind him that You love him, Lord,
And wash away the stain.

My pastor asked for helpers
To make some calls today.
Though I can't go—I'd love to—
Lord, lead them as I pray.

In distant lands men long for peace.
They've never heard of You.
Oh, send someone to tell them
That they can know You too.

It seems that I do so little
As I amble along with my crutch,
But help me today as I try to pray
The prayer that availeth much.

—Margaret Primrose

Our Changing World

Through every change in our lives,
Through each phase or endeavor,
God is with us giving strength,
His comfort and wisdom, forever.

The faith we need, the promise of hope
In His hands He holds the assurance
For a changing world
As each life unfolds.

We thank You, God, for the love
That to us You are sending;
May we face our changing world
With a love that is unending.

"Therefore will not we fear, though the earth be removed, and though the mountains be carried into the midst of the sea" (Psalm 46:2).

—Helen Kitchell Evans

My Prayer for Each Day

To those I love
may I be a little kinder.
To the faults of others
may I be a little blinder.
Lord, may I still be
a little bit more cheery,
Though with trials and tribulations
I may become very, very weary.
Help me make someone's life a little sweeter
by the things I do or say
Is my prayer
for every day.

—Helen Kitchell Evans

Grandpa

Bedtime for me was special
When we went to Grandpa's farm;
Each night he told me stories
With his fascinating charm.

He spoke of many thrillers
Of courageous pioneers,
Of Indians and hardships,
Covered wagons, bleak frontiers.

He was tenderly concerned
With my problems and my cares,
As Grandpas should be; he took my side,
And he listened to my prayers.

One night he gently covered me
With a blanket, soft and warm
And stretched out right beside me
So I wouldn't fear a storm.

The lightning flashed, the thunder roared,
His voice grew louder and deep.
But he soon tired, and closed his eyes . . .
Ha! Grandpa was asleep!

The years have passed by quickly.
Priceless truth I now can see.
I'm so glad when God made grandpas
That He gave this one to me!

—Lillian Pittman

READINGS, SKETCHES, AND SERVICE HELPS

A Dedication for a Retiree

A Choral Reading upon the Celebration of Retirement

by Faye Nyce

CONGREGATION: "The LORD will fulfill his purpose for me; your steadfast love, O LORD, endures forever. Do not forsake the work of your hands." [Psalm 138:8, NRSV*]

PASTOR: You [or name of retiree] have come to a crossroad in your life. The past is a chapter that was at times exciting, humdrum, fulfilling, and rewarding. That chapter is now closed. It is time to go to the next chapter; to eagerly delve into what the Lord has in store for you at this time.

RETIREE: As I look back, I have had many blessings. There are also memories of decisions I wish I had made in a different way. Yet, I have the satisfaction of knowing I did what seemed best with the knowledge I had at the time.

PASTOR: Such sentiments are common to everyone. We have a great God who knows this and accepts us as we are when we are genuinely seeking to follow Him. Psalm 139 tells us that the Lord has searched us and knows every word even before we speak it. Yet, He desires to claim us for His own.

CONGREGATION: The Lord knows both the way you have already trod, as well as the road before you. He will not forsake you.

RETIREE: I have the confidence that God is creative, and He can open any door He desires for my future ministry. God will finish the work.

CONGREGATION: You are one of us, and we will continue to stand by you.

PASTOR: Jesus says, "I chose you." He will not abandon one in whom He delights. God's blessing will rest upon you.

(PASTOR *closes with a prayer of thanksgiving for the life lived, appealing to the Lord for the retiree's future.)*

Letter from Grandma

by Juanita Killough Urbach

In that interval between Grandma Water's death and her funeral, family members decided to clean out her apartment at the retirement village. It was an emotional time as we sorted through her intimate belongings. In the process, we found a small box of mementos with the names of each intended recipient attached. One letter was addressed to me. With shaking hands, I opened it and began to read.

Dear Ann,

My dear, you are very special to me and because you are, I have to try one more time to tell you what lays so heavily on my heart. I'm concerned about where you are going to spend eternity.

Of all of my grandchildren, you are the only one I'm not sure about. All the others have made a public confession of faith.

Every time I tried to talk to you about it, you always said, "Later."

By the time you read this, I won't be around to keep reminding you. So for that reason, I'm uneasy and hesitant to leave you. I wish I could make you understand that time runs out for all of us. We don't even know if there will be a tomorrow.

I first learned that when I went to a camp meeting and heard an evangelist say, "Jesus is coming back again. It could be today!"

He quoted scriptures that gave signs of what to look for. I can't remember them all, but one stands out in my mind. It was a comparison to the days of Noah. People were eating, drinking, marrying, and giving in marriage right up to the day of the flood. He spoke of wars and rumors of wars, of nations rising up against one another. And then he warned that false prophets would appear and deceive many.

I was scared. I knew I was a sinner, and I didn't want to be left behind when Jesus came. The very thought of Judgment Day—when the saints and sinners will be divided; the saints join the Lord in heaven and the sinners sent to a burning hell—was overwhelming. I knew I didn't want to go to hell.

I rushed to the altar with tears streaming down my face. I prayed, asking God for forgiveness. I knew He had answered my prayer when suddenly I felt light as if a great load had been lifted off my shoulders. I stood up and told everyone that Jesus had saved me.

From that day, I began looking for Jesus to return. I thought because some of the signs had already happened the rest would surely happen in my lifetime.

After I finished high school, I went away to a Christian college where I met your grandfather. He was studying for the ministry. Years passed, we got married and raised our family in parsonages of the various churches he pastored. Together, we watched and waited, expecting Jesus to return and claim His own. Even after your grandfather went to heaven, I still thought I might live to see that day.

I'm sure according to what's happening all around us, Jesus could come at any time. But now, I find myself praying that He wait just a little longer. I don't want you to miss heaven. My uppermost desire is for us to be presented to the Heavenly Father as a family. One by one, the others have come to know Jesus as their Savior. But like the shepherd in the parable, I'm concerned about the one who is lost.

In my lifetime I've had to learn patience. It isn't one of my virtues. I hate to wait and especially when I see signs of prophecy being fulfilled. I get anxious.

But now that my time is running out, I have to accept that Jesus is also waiting. I'm sure He is hoping more sinners will repent before it is too late. And I have to agree if just one more soul is saved from a burning hell on that final Day of Judgment, it will justify the wait.

Yes, my child, I'm praying that you will heed His call and mend your ways. I love you. I want to share heaven with you. I'm not sure what to expect in that glorious place, but if we are together, I will be happy. So once again, I'm pleading with you.

I hope this letter will convince you that the time is short. Look around you and see for yourself. Jesus could come at any minute. Please get ready.

Love,
Grandma

Grandma, dear sweet Grandma. You never gave up. Even when you faced death, you were still thinking about me. I'm ashamed to think of the anxiety I must have caused you. I didn't mean to. Truly, I didn't. I always knew you were right, but I wasn't ready to make a commitment. I thought I could have all the world offered first and then seek God's forgiveness in time to make it to heaven.

When you talked about the Lord's return to earth, I envisioned it to be a long way in the future. Such talk made me uneasy. That's why I always said, "Later."

But now I see that it is dangerous to wait. Death could strike at any moment. Even you, Grandma, had no choice in that matter. You couldn't wait for me, and I don't want to be left behind like the foolish virgins with no oil in my lamp.

Please, God, forgive me and help me to be the person Grandma envisioned me to be. Help me to pattern myself after her. Keep my heart and mind centered on You until the end of time.

You out there, take a lesson from me. Don't procrastinate. God is gracious, good, and kind, but He won't wait forever.

One of these days the eastern sky will split and King Jesus will come down from heaven on a cloud of glory to gather the saints to himself. Grandma will be there, and we will be reunited. I can hardly wait!

Grandma's Window

by Grace Olson Pulham

As I looked out my large kitchen window I saw two of my grandchildren coming down the road. When they drew near they waved at me and announced that they wanted to see my day-old chicks. I told them that they couldn't go into the chicken coop but would have to look at them through the window.

Fourteen-year-old Jenny and four-year-old Christopher looked at the chicks and then came to the house. They visited with me for a few minutes and then Christopher said, "I'm going outside. He looked at me through the window and said, "Hi, Grandma," as he waved his pudgy little hand.

Jenny's gray eyes shone as she flipped her dark brown, waist-length hair over her shoulder and declared, "I'll go see Grandma through the window too." She went out, took Christopher by the hand, turned, and said, "Bye, Grandma," and they went back up the road.

I became thoughtful as my grandchildren disappeared toward home. Many times my family had waved at me as they saw me through my kitchen window. My grandson waved at me when he went by on the tractor; the others looked for me when going by my house.

Much of my work is done in the kitchen. Not only cooking, baking, and eating, but writing, reading, and other tasks are performed near the big front window.

That day I began checking my attitudes and motivations to see if I could see what my grandchildren see as they look through the window of my heart. Do they see Christ there? Does my everyday life show them what it is to be a true child of God? Am I showing them real love? Am I helping them by example to be Christlike? I believe children perceive more than we realize, if a person is real or fake.

I've had a chance to look through my grandma's window. I have her Bible with all her markings and clippings still there.

Soon after my grandchildren's visit, I came across the scripture in Titus 2:2 and 3. "That the aged men be sober, grave, temperate, sound in faith, in charity, in patience. The aged women likewise, that they be in behaviour as becometh holiness, not false accusers, not given to much wine, teachers of good things." These are the things I want my grandchildren to see through Grandma's window.

I've been different things to different people; pastor's wife, mother, church pianist, child evangelist, guest speaker, but none of these jobs is more important than being "Grandma's window."

The Perfect Church

by Annette Dake

Cast:

MILDRED
FRED

Prop:

Lady's purse.

Setting:

A pew in a typical church.

(As the scene opens, MILDRED *is already seated in the pew. Her purse is beside her in the adjacent seat.* FRED *walks in briskly, as if he's a bit late.)*

FRED: Morning, Mildred. A good Lord's Day to you. *(He picks up the purse and hands it to her.)* What's with the purse in my seat?

MILDRED *(whispering):* I had to save your place.

FRED: Save my place? Mildred, what are you talking about? This has been our pew since 1951!

MILDRED: I know, I know. But last week some *visitor* tried to sit down right here! Can you imagine the nerve?

FRED: Visitor? (MILDRED *nods.)* Who let him in?

MILDRED: You know who. That young pup, Pastor Sims. Honestly, always inviting new people here. To *our* church!

FRED *(shaking his head):* Trying to sit in our pew. What's this church coming to?

MILDRED: That's not all. Guess what else happened this morning?

FRED: Deacon Thomas finally cut the tag off his toupee? *(Laughs)*

MILDRED: No. Just before you came, Effie Mae Hodges walked right over and talked to me.

FRED: Effie Mae Hodges! Why, you two haven't spoken in, what—15 years?

MILDRED: Seventeen years next month. Strange, isn't it? It's been so long, I've even forgotten what I was mad about. I think it had something to do with her cat in my petunias . . .

FRED: You're picking daisies again, Mildred. *(Pause)* What did Effie Mae want?

MILDRED: She invited me to her house for coffee on Tuesday.

FRED: Why on earth for?

MILDRED: Said she wanted to "bury the hatchet."

FRED: In your back, most likely! *(Laughs)*

MILDRED: More to do with that whippersnapper's sermons, I bet. Always meddling where he doesn't belong. Always preaching *(snootily)* love and forgiveness. Whatever happened to hellfire and sin, I'd like to know?

FRED: Yeah! Sin and hellfire were always good enough for us!

MILDRED: Exactly.

FRED *(taps* MILDRED *on the arm):* Well, will you look at that?

MILDRED: Can you believe Abigail would wear a dress like that?

FRED: Looks like my old, overstuffed chair I'm so fond of.

MILDRED: If she tries to sing those high notes today, I'll bet we'll see more stuffin' than chair.

FRED: You don't think she'll try one of them Sandi Peppermint Patti songs, do you?

MILDRED: Probably. She's such a show-off. I don't know why she tries to sing. I have perfect pitch myself you know, and I can hear every sour note that woman hits.

FRED: Mildred, why don't you ever sing?

MILDRED: Why, I wouldn't want people talking about me. You know how *some* people are—always complaining about something.

FRED: Yeah. What's this church coming to?

MILDRED: Oh, great. Here comes little Mr. Sammy Sunshine.

FRED: Mr. Prayer in the Flesh. Why does Pastor always call on him to pray? I can pray. I can say all those "thees" and "thys" and all that "thuff" . . . uh . . . stuff.

MILDRED: I know, Fred. Don't worry yourself. You know Pastor Sims has favorites. How Sam always prays for other people *(snootily again)*—the sick ones, the hurt ones, the messed-up-in-the-head ones. All the deadbeats of the world. Have you ever once heard him pray for me and my rheumatism?

FRED: Or my bunions?

MILDRED: Exactly!

FRED: Mercy, what's this church comin' to?

MILDRED: And there he is? Pastor Sims, ready for another love-in.

FRED: Wonder what he'll preach about today? Could it be . . . love your brother . . . or love one another, or maybe a new twist, greater love hath no man . . .

MILDRED: The prodigal son. I can't believe it. Didn't he preach that one already?

FRED: Glorifying a young man that squanders his daddy's life savings, comes crawling back home, Daddy sets out the finest china . . . is that the one?

MILDRED: Yep. And you know what? I always sympathized with that other brother. There he worked and worked, while Junior lived it up. Then Junior comes sniveling back, and other brother gets a talkin' to. That's what happens when you preach love and forget burn!

FRED: Mercy, mercy, what's this church comin' to?

MILDRED: Maybe he'll keep it short this morning. My rheumatism's acting up. Oh, but then there's his favorite time each week. Pastor Sims beggin' people to come to the altar. Why do we have to have an invitation every service?

FRED: I think he's trying to keep a head count. I can see it now in next week's bulletin. "Fifteen Souls Saved Last Week." Praise the Lord and pass the Kleenex.

MILDRED: Head count. That's what he's a-doin'. You're so smart, Fred. Uh, oh! Here we go! Offering. Hold on to your change purse.

FRED: Count on it like clockwork. That offering plate comes around more than my mother-in-law.

MILDRED: They're just trying to pay for that new Outreach Center they want to build. I could use a little outreach, couldn't you, Fred? All they're gonna do is build that thing for the young people.

FRED: What's this church comin' to?

MILDRED: Be friendly. Why does he always say be friendly? Just once I'd like to hear him say, "Be yourself!"

FRED: Church just isn't what it used to be in the good ol' days, is it, Mildred? What's this church comin' to?

MILDRED: Don't worry yourself, Fred. We'll just have to trust the good Lord!

FRED: Guess you're right, Mildred! Well, I'll see you next Sunday. God bless you!

MILDRED: God bless you, Fred.

FRED *(as he exits):* What's this church comin' to?

To Paint like the Master

by Jamie J. Puckett

Cast:

Martha
Mary

Props:

Two canvases, an easel, several paintbrushes, a golf bag.
Other "props" may be mimed.

Setting:

Mary and Martha's busy art studio in a museum.

(As the scene opens, Martha *is busily painting on a canvas and* Mary *is watching. The painting does not face the audience.)*

Martha: Well, I'm almost finished. What do you think?

Mary: That's some of your best work yet. I can really see a resemblance to a painting by, dare I say it, Vidal Aristotle?

Martha: Oh, Mary. That's the most I could hope for. That's the ultimate. His brushstrokes. His precision. His passion.

Mary: Oh yes. He must have such depth of soul. The shapes he uses redefine . . . shapes.

Martha: I would give anything to learn from him—to just watch him paint.

Mary: Me too. *(She hears something going on offstage.)* Hey, what's going on downstairs in the lecture hall?

Martha: I don't know. There must be a guest speaker today. Why don't you go see who it is.

Mary: OK. (Mary *leaves for a moment as* Martha *continues painting.* Mary *rushes back in.)* Martha! Martha! Martha! You'll never believe it! It's him. It's *(a harsh whisper as if afraid saying his name will make him go away)* . . . Vidal Aristotle. He's here!

Martha: The Great Master? The King of Chromotism? The Sheik of Shapes? He's here?

Mary: He's right downstairs. I think he's going to paint.

MARTHA: Oh no—that's too much. I need some water.

(MARTHA *looks around the room searching for something to drink. She seizes upon a glass with paintbrushes soaking. She removes the brushes and drinks the dirty water.)*

MARY: Well, come on. Let's go down there.

MARTHA: In a minute. I want my painting to be finished when Vidal Aristotle sees it. It's got to be just right.

MARY: Well, OK. But, hurry up. He's starting.

MARTHA: I will. Save me a place.

MARY: OK. *(Exits)*

MARTHA: Oh, I hope he notices that I have patterned my texture after his. I think he'll be honored. Oh! *(She has messed up. She frantically looks around for a damp cloth.)* Turpentine, turpentine. *(She finds it and dabs it on the painting.)* There. I think that's good. I hope he likes it. I'd better hurry, so I can see him. *(She starts to leave, but notices the studio and hesitates.)* Oh, just look at this place. My studio is a sty! What will he think? I've got to clean this place up.

MARY *(rushes back in):* Martha. You're missing it. What are you doing?

MARTHA: I'm trying to clean up this st . . . our studio, and I think you should be in here helping me.

MARY: Come on, Martha. He doesn't care if our studio is a little messy.

MARTHA: Oh yes, he does. You remember that quote in *Landscape Today* where he said "a clean studio is the key to a clean soul."

MARY: Yeah, but he's painting . . . downstairs . . . right now. And I'm going to see him. *(Exits)*

MARTHA *(pouting to herself as she putters around cleaning up):* Fine, then. Go ahead. Some sister. Leave me in here to do all the work. Just go. I'll clean this place up by myself. And when Vidal Aristotle comes in and asks who keeps this place so tidy, we'll just see who'll be smiling then. There, that's good. I'm ready. *(Starts to leave)* Wait. If he comes back here for a little reception, then we'll need a bunch of hors d'oeuvres and little sandwiches and cheese wedgies and . . .

MARY *(dashing back in):* Martha, do you know what he said? He said that "a paintbrush is to a painter what a pitchfork is to a farmer." Isn't that profound? *(Dashes back out)*

MARTHA: That is so profound. That is the most profound thing I have ever heard. OK . . . little sandwiches. *(Showing her bitterness)* Who does she think she is, just running off and sitting around while I'm taking care of all the work. *(Looks through imaginary cabinets)* What'd she do with the tuna? Where's the peanut butter? I bet she took it. Oh, here it is. *No!* There's not much left. I work my fingers to the bone, and my sister eats all the peanut butter. That's not fair. Why doesn't she get in here and help me? *(Begins to make sandwiches)* Of all the ungrateful people in the world, I get her for a sister. *(Rapidly makes the rest of the sandwiches and cuts them up)* There! OK, the sandwiches are ready. My painting is complete. The studio is spotless. Everything is ready. Vidal Aristotle, here I come. *(She exits.)*

(After a moment, VIDAL *and* MARY *enter from the other side. They are in the midst of a conversation.* VIDAL *is all flourish and fruity.)*

VIDAL: That's what I'm talking about—lighting! Color! Texture! This is the key! You must use the brush strokes to express your emotion. *(He spies the painting and the easel. Gives it a once-over. Turns it this way and that, gives a kind of shrug to indicate that it's not bad. Puts it aside and puts up another canvas. He whips out a brush like a sword from his belt loop.)* Today, I'm feeling light and fluffy *(he begins to paint)*—fluff, fluff, fluff, and voilà! *(He slams the brush down on the easel or in a glass.)* I'm finished. It's a masterpiece. *(He turns the painting around. It is something simple like a smiley face and a triangle, or something artsy like that.)* And now, I must go. I have a 1:00 tee-time on the lawns.

MARY *(to the audience):* He drinks tea, and he's not even afraid to admit it. What a man!

VIDAL: Drink tea? I'm talking about golf. *(He picks up the bag of clubs that is hidden somehow.)* I'm supposed to meet my foursome, and I'm late. *(Exits)*

MARY *(as* MARTHA *enters):* He's . . . brilliant.

MARTHA: Mary?

MARY: He's . . . beautiful.

MARTHA: Where is he?

MARY: He's . . . gone.

MARTHA: Gone . . . like the wind.

MARTHA: I missed it?

MARY: You missed it.

MARTHA: Vidal Aristotle was here, and I missed it?

MARY: Yep.

MARTHA: You ungrateful little whelp. Why didn't you come and help me. If you had, I could have had this place ready in no time, and I could have seen him too.

MARY: I don't know. I just wanted to see him paint—to learn from his wisdom, his compassion, his . . . his . . . his brushstrokes.

MARTHA: Well if he's mister all-knowing, all-compassionate, master-painter, then why didn't he know I was up here slaving away and send you up to help. *He* could have made you come help me.

(VIDAL *reenters. He has been listening to the conversation.)*

VIDAL: Excuse me. I came back for my brushes. I couldn't help overhearing. You know, Martha, you are worried about too many things. You missed out on the thing that was most important. The things you were doing were all good, but Mary knew that the best way to learn to paint like the master is to watch the master paint. She chose the most important thing. And, it shall not be taken away from her. *(He starts to leave, then stops in front of* MARY. *He gives her the paintbrush.)* Use it, Mary—paint! Paint like the master.

(All freeze. Then MARTHA *[out of character] steps forward. She quotes Luke 10:38-42.)*

Stop and Wonder Why

by Lora Lee Curtiss

Cast:

LEAF *(one person or a small chorus)*
READER *(one or more)*
TWO GOSSIPS
LEAF TURNERS *(nonspeaking role)*

Props:

A small tree decorated with construction paper leaves. On one prominent branch the leaves should be green on one side and yellow on the other. These should be loosely tied with yarn so that they can be easily untied and turned.

Setting:

A tree. All leaves are turned to the green.

Suggested Use: As part of a fall banquet. Invitation can be written on colored paper leaves

LEAF: I am a leaf. I've only lived on this tree a few short months, but it seems a lifetime. I don't live alone. There are thousands just like me on this same tree. Sometimes, I feel insignificant. Just one bit of matter occupying a speck of space between the sky above and the earth below.

READER *(enters):* How about you? Do you, too, feel insignificant? Do you have the same feeling of "What can I do? I'm only one among so many?"

LEAF: Brrrrr. A chilly wind blows at me. The branch is so noisy and crowded with everybody twisting and turning. Hey, Wind, stop it. You're shaking the whole tree. I'm glad my stem is so sturdy and strong.

READER: What is shaking your tree? Family problems? Unemployment? Retirement? Loneliness? Do you have a stem of faith that is strong enough when trouble comes?

LEAF: My neighbor is pestering me. Every time he moves close he shrieks in my ear. It sounds as if he is hollering, "Help!" What does he expect? I have all I can do to take care of myself. So I shriek at him, "Stay in your own place." Then the horrible happens. I watch as he suddenly lets go. Without a sound, he slips out of sight. I call out, "I'm sorry. Come back. I'll help you." But it's too late. He vanishes in the night, leaving only a tiny empty space where he had lived out his whole life. Shall I never see him again?

READER: Do you hear the cries of those who call out to you? Do you turn away from those who need help? Do you hear? Do you care?

LEAF: At last, the tree quiets down. I take a deep breath and once again from the top of this marvelous tree the world and all I see belongs to me, me, me.

(LEAF TURNERS *enter, untie, and turn the leaves on one branch.)*

LEAF: Many cycles of light and dark have come and gone. And though the sun shines brightly, it doesn't seem to warm me. I don't feel well. I'm so thirsty. "Water, water, I need water, I cry." But no one hears such as I.

READER: Think about those who occupy the tree where you live. Are the young acting obnoxiously because their supply of nourishing love is being cut off? Are the elderly suffering pangs of loneliness and depression because they have lost contact with love-giving people?

LEAF: I feel weak and dry. The leaves crackle with news. I strain to listen.

FIRST GOSSIPER: Did you hear about the family on the north branch?

SECOND GOSSIPER: Well, I did hear they were asked to move.

FIRST GOSSIPER: Not asked, my dear. They were evicted. I heard it from my cousin who is a very good friend of . . .

SECOND GOSSIPER: Never mind that. I'm dying to hear what happened.

FIRST GOSSIPER: Don't tell another leaf, but I heard that they turned colors. At first, no one really noticed, but they all turned a shocking yellow. And you know we never have had folks of color on this tree. Not ever as long as I have been here. Just think what the neighborhood will become.

SECOND GOSSIPER: Shocking. I shudder to think what I would do if it happened on our branch. We are all such a pretty shade. Just right. We all belong.

(LEAF TURNERS *enter and turn the leaves of* GOSSIP*'s branch to yellow. Much to the shock and amazement of the* GOSSIPS.)

READER: Do you judge others by their color? Do you wrap yourself in a blanket of self-righteousness and snub those whose skin is a different shade from yours?

LEAF: Why don't I see the sun anymore? Why is the sky always gray? Oh, no, here comes that awful wind again. I can't hold on. My stem is breaking loose. I'm falling! I'm falling. But wait. No. The wind is my friend. It's carrying me up higher and higher. I'm floating. I'm flying. I'm free. Look. I'm even higher than Mother Tree. She looks so different from up here. I can't believe it. She's all yellow. And what are those little creatures doing down there. Running and jumping. Wait, I'm floating down, down, down. I hit the ground. Unprotected, unloved, just a bit of chaff I become that the wind drives away. I am no more.

READER: Even when the leaf dies and lies decomposing on the ground, it is an important part of the cycle of life. By returning to the soil it releases nutrients that are vital if life on this planet is to continue. We, too, belong to this wondrous chain. But, we are different from the leaf. We can stop and wonder why. We can reach out to those who cry.

When We Were Young(er)

by Margaret Primrose

One of the simplest and oldest uses of questions like these would be to read some of them to contestants, let them write their answers, and then check their papers. The persons with the highest score would appreciate a prize.

You may also use these questions to make up games similar to Wheel of Fortune, Ticktacktoe, Trivial Pursuit, or Captain, May I? Or remembering an old-fashioned spelling bee may help you think of a new game.

Many familiar games including Ticktacktoe and Captain, May I? will adapt to the use of two teams with captains who can appeal to their teammates for help. In some cases you may need a chalkboard the group can watch. If you wish, the number of points per question may vary with the difficulty of the question.

Questions on Music

(Quotes are all from KJV.)

1. Finish this quotation: "Serve the LORD with gladness: ______________. *(come before his presence with singing" [Psalm 100:2].)*

2. Who wrote the words to the poem and hymn "Crossing the Bar," which begins with these words, "Sunset and evening star, / And one clear call for me"? *(Alfred Tennyson)*

3. What spiritual about the Israelites' cry to leave Egyptian bondage took on parallel meaning for Afro-American slaves in the United States? *("Go Down, Moses")*

4. According to an old song, where did Daisy's boyfriend think she would look sweet on their wedding day? *(On a bicycle built for two)*

5. What holiday is associated with *Amahl and the Night Visitors,* which premiered on American television in 1951? *(Christmas)*

6. What still-popular hymn was written by a sea captain converted during a storm? *("Amazing Grace" by John Newton)*

7. The title of this song tells us about something that was good for Paul and Silas, the Hebrew children and our fathers. What was it? *("The Old-time Religion")*

8. What song points out that neither sun, moon, flowers, robins nor sunbeams cost us anything? *("The Best Things in Life Are Free")*

9. Ethel Waters loved this song from childhood and sang it to her dying grandmother as well as to large audiences.
("His Eye Is on the Sparrow")

10. The famous evangelist Homer Rodeheaver used this as his theme song, but it talks to adults as well as children about letting their light shine in obscure places.
("Brighten the Corner Where You Are")

Questions on Bible Characters

1. What praying woman was thought to be drunk?
(Hannah—1 Samuel 1:13)

2. Identify Obed.
(He was the grandfather of David and also the son of Ruth and Boaz—Ruth 4:1-17.)

3. How did sailors on board the ship with Jonah learn that he was running away from the Lord?
(Jonah told them—Jonah 1:10.)

4. How old was Abraham, father of the faithful, when his wife Sarah gave birth to Isaac?
(He was 100 years old—Genesis 17:17.)

5. What was Paul's hometown?
(Tarsus. He had been called Saul of Tarsus.)

6. What was the name of the queen Esther replaced?
(Vashti—Esther 1)

7. Name the king God called "a man after my own heart."?
(David—Acts 13:22)

8. The first part of this man's name will make you think of a building on a farm.
*(**Barn**abas)*

9. The middle part of what Philistine woman's name is a sin spoken against in the Ten Commandments?
*(De**li**lah—Exodus 20:16)*

10. Moses asked Pharaoh when to entreat for the frogs plaguing the Egyptians to be destroyed. What answer did Pharaoh give?
(Tomorrow—Exodus 8:8-10)

11. Which three of Jesus' disciples witnessed the Transfiguration?
(Peter, James, and John—Matthew 17:1)

12. How old was Caleb when Moses chose him as one of the spies to go into the Promised Land?
(40 years old—Joshua 14:7)

13. How old was Caleb when he received Hebron as his inheritance?
(85 years old—Joshua 14:10-14)

14. How many years did Methuselah live?
(969—Genesis 5:27)

Questions on This and That

1. What is another name for rhubarb?
(Pie plant)

2. What is "devil's rope" and what use do farmers make of it?
(Barbed wired used for fences)

3. People don't usually eat cranberries and popcorn together. At what season did yesterday's children combine them and why?
(They used to string them for Christmas tree decorations.)

4. Name the inexpensive green or pink glassware that has become a collectible.
(Depression glass)

5. In what decade was the bikini swimsuit introduced?
(1940—1950)

6. Which of these was rationed, not just hard to find, during World War II: sugar, women's hosiery, canned pineapple?
(Sugar)

7. Name three ingredients you would need for chess pie?
(Butter, sugar, eggs, cornmeal, lemon juice or vinegar, flour, lard)

8. What would you do with something "larruping good"?
(Eat it. Sorghum was one of the things that was sometimes called larruping good.)

9. What name was given to the women's fashions designed by Christian Dior in 1947? Featured were long, full skirts and narrow shoulders.
(The New Look)

10. Though such things as food and clothing are necessities, the Bible teaches that life consisteth not in ______________________________.
(the abundance of the things we possess—Luke 12:15)

Questions from the News

1. What did President Franklin Roosevelt say was a date that would live in infamy?
(The December 7, 1941, bombing of Pearl Harbor)

2. What American general received the Japanese surrender on the U.S.S. *Missouri* on September 2, 1945?
(General Douglas MacArthur)

3. Who was Erwin Rommel?
(A German general active in battles in North Africa during World War II)

4. How many home runs did Babe Ruth hit in his career?
(714)

5. In what year before the Great Depression did the stock market crash?
(1929)

6. What was the name of the airplane that made the first nonstop flight across the Atlantic and who was the pilot?
(Charles Lindbergh flew the Spirit of St. Louis.)

7. What statesman stoutly declared that he and his "Island" would defend themselves at whatever cost, including blood, sweat, and tears?
(Winston Churchill)

8. Name three of the five Dionne quintuplets, born in Canada over 60 years ago.
(Marie, Annette, Cecile, Yvonne, Emilie)

9. Who was president when Billy Sunday died in 1935?
(Franklin Roosevelt)

10. For what is John Dillinger (1903-34) remembered?
(He was considered as one of the most notorious criminals in U.S. history.)

11. What does Proverbs 10:27 say will happen to the years of the wicked?
(They shall be shortened.)

Questions on Literature

1. Who was the author of *O, Pioneers* and *My Antonia,* which depict life on the Great Plains?
(Willa Cather)

2. Name the man who terrified thousands with his radio broadcast of *The War of the Worlds* in 1938.
(Orson Welles)

3. What is the title of the controversial novel written by John Steinbeck to portray Depression-Era America?
(The Grapes of Wrath)

4. Where would you find these words: "We hold these truths to be self-evident, that all men were created equal, that they are endowed by their Creator with certain unalienable rights, that among these are life, liberty, and the pursuit of happiness"?
(The Declaration of Independence)

5. In *The Merchant of Venice* one of William Shakespeare's characters talked about never having known a body with so old a ________. Supply the missing word.
(Head)

6. What did Daniel Webster say are now and forever inseparable?
(Liberty and union)

7. In *Rabbi Ben Ezra* Robert Browning asked the reader to grow old along with him. What did he say was yet to be?
(The best)

8. In Psalm 119:105 the psalmist used two symbols for God's Word. What are they?
("A lamp unto my feet and a light unto my path")

Questions on the Economy

1. According to 1 Timothy 5:9, how old did a needy and righteous widow have to be before she could receive the "social security" of her day?
(60)

2. Who did Rosie the Riveter symbolize?
(Women who went to work during World War II to help build such things as cargo ships and planes.)

3. How much would you have had to pay in 1964 to mail a one-page letter from one point in the United States to another?
(5 cents)

4. During the Great Depression years, if a farmer's wife did not have coal or wood for her cookstove, what is one thing she might have had to use?
(Corn cobs, or ears of corn; paper; cow chips [dried manure]; hay)

5. What was a typical beginning salary for government employees in Washington, D.C., when the Japanese bombed Pearl Harbor?
($1,440 a year [credit should be given if a contestant comes within $200 of it.])

6. During the Great Depression, how might a housewife who did her own baking acquire enough fabric for her daughter's school dresses?
(From printed flour sacks)

7. If a person during the Great Depression told you that he was working for PWA, what organization would he have meant?
(Public Works Administration created by the government for the jobless)

8. Finish this verse: "I have been young, and now am old; yet have I not seen the righteous ________________________________.
(forsaken, nor his seed begging bread" [Psalm 37:25].)

Questions on Vehicles and Etc.

1. Repeat the following in the order in which they appeared on the market: Model A Ford; Ford V-8, Model T Ford; Ford Taurus.
(Model T, Model A, V-8, Taurus)

2. If you were riding in a rumble seat, where would you be: under a boxcar of a moving train; in a horse-drawn buggy, in a seat that folded from the trunk of a car?
(In the seat that folded from the car's trunk)

3. Match these brands names—Lionel, Effanbee, and Ball—with the products, dolls, canning jars, and toy trains.
(Lionel, trains; Effanbee, dolls; Ball, canning jars)

4. For what was a B-17 used?
(It was an American "Flying Fortress" airplane used for bombing during World War II.)

5. Before the days of combines to harvest wheat, oats, and other small grains, which two machines did farmers use in harvesting?
(Binders and threshing machines)

6. What automobile that is no longer being made shared the name with a bay that indents east central Canada?
(Hudson)

7. If you say you have a "Seth Thomas," would you be referring to a clock, a vacuum cleaner, or a hand-cranked ice cream freezer?
(Clock)

8. If the "Raleigh man" still came to your door to peddle, which might you buy from him—seed corn, vanilla, or tools?
(Vanilla)

9. Suppose you're dreaming of inventing something and finish this verse: "Your sons and your daughters shall prophesy, your old men shall ____________, your young men shall ______________."
(dream dreams; see visions—Joel 2:28)

Questions on Entertainment (Including Sports)

1. What Afro-American contralto was denied the opportunity to sing at Constitution Hall in Washington, D.C., in 1938?
(Marian Anderson)

2. What did Charlie McCarthy, Edgar Bergen, Fred Allen, and Jack Benny have in common?
(They were radio comedians before the days of television.)

3. For what is Norwegian-born Sonja Henie remembered?
(Ice skating)

4. How did actor Will Rogers die?
(With Wiley Post in a plane crash near Point Barrow, Alaska)

5. If King Solomon lived today and said the same thing he did about the pleasures of his day, what would we hear?
(That they are vanity—Ecclesiastes 2.)

6. With what sport was Mickey Mantle associated?
(Baseball)

7. What couple used "Happy Trails" for their radio show and in public appearances?
(Dale Evans and Roy Rogers)

A ONE-ACT PLAY

The Lord's Not Finished with Us Yet!

by Paul McCusker
(From *Snapshots and Portraits,* by Paul McCusker
published by Lillenas Publishing Company)

(A rest home. MAUDE, *an elderly woman wheels* JOSHUA *in his wheelchair onstage, and positions him facing the audience.* JOSHUA *has had a stroke and cannot talk. His thoughts can be communicated in several ways. One is to cover* JOSHUA's *lips with a large, old-fashioned, walrus-type mustache. He can "talk his thoughts" with minimal interference or distraction. Another possibility is to take "dramatic license" and let him talk directly to the audience [with little or no physical movement except for his lips and eyes]. Or there is always the dubbing of his the lines in over the PA system.)*

MAUDE: There you go, Joshua.

JOSHUA *(thinking):* Why does she keep bringing me here? I hate this view.

MAUDE: Your favorite spot. You can see the entire back lawn from here, can't you?

JOSHUA *(thinking):* Great. Weeds, old people, and the cemetery. I hate this view.

MAUDE: Look, there's Ralph and Andrew playing croquet. How nice. I do admire that kind of perseverance. Y'know, Ralph had a stroke last time he played. Oh, I'm sorry. I shouldn't mention the word "stroke." I mean, since you had yours . . . and you can't move or talk . . . I wanna be sensitive.

JOSHUA *(thinking):* Good going, Maude. Why don't you go haunt some other hospital? *(Growls)* Volunteers.

MAUDE *(holds up an envelope):* Lookie what I have, Joshua. *(She waves it in front of his face slowly.)* It's an envelope. It's addressed to you: Mr. Joshua Forbes. I wonder what's in it?

JOSHUA *(thinking):* Oh, brother.

MAUDE: Is it a letter? Maybe it's a card!

JOSHUA *(thinking):* Maybe it's a cure for senility. Get on with it, Maude.

MAUDE *(opens the envelope):* It is a card! A *birthday* card. *(Knowingly)* I wonder who's birthday it is? Do *you* know?

JOSHUA *(thinking):* I thought "Romper Room" got canceled.

MAUDE: It's *your* birthday, Joshua!

JOSHUA *(thinking):* Read the card, Maude.

MAUDE: Congratulations. How old are you?

(He looks at her puzzled, not knowing how to communicate an answer.)

JOSHUA *(thinking):* What do you want me to do—stamp like a horse?

MAUDE: You must be at least 85.

JOSHUA *(thinking):* And you look like a million, Maude. Read the card.

MAUDE: Well, now—what does this lovely card say? Oh, look . . . *(Shows him the front of the card, then yanks it away before he can look)* Flowers.

JOSHUA *(thinking):* How tacky.

MAUDE: How pretty.

JOSHUA *(thinking):* Gotta be from Jim. He always picks tacky cards.

MAUDE: It's from . . . *(looks inside)* your son, Jim. It says, "For a wonderful father on his birthday . . ."

JOSHUA *(thinking):* I like funny birthday cards. I just hope it's not one of those cards that tries to rhyme.

MAUDE: On the inside, it says: "God bless you on your special day / For what you do, for what you say . . ."

JOSHUA *(thinking):* Oh, brother.

MAUDE: "May you find true happiness / And all your birthday wishes get."

JOSHUA *(thinking):* "Happiness" and "get" don't rhyme.

MAUDE: "Love, Jim."

JOSHUA *(thinking):* Did he enclose a check?

MAUDE *(puts envelope away):* How sweet.

JOSHUA *(thinking):* For a card like that, he should've enclosed a check.

MAUDE: A card like that must make your birthday special.

JOSHUA *(thinking):* I'd rather get a plane ticket to Hawaii.

MAUDE *(begins to cry):* Oh, Joshua . . .

JOSHUA *(thinking):* Oh, Maude, please don't start.

MAUDE: It breaks my heart to see you like this.

JOSHUA *(thinking):* See me like *what?*

MAUDE: I hope I never have a stroke.

JOSHUA *(thinking):* Eh. Could be worse. I mean, it's like an old car. The body's fallin' apart, but the motor's in great shape.

MAUDE: All you can do is sit there.

JOSHUA *(thinking):* And listen to you.

MAUDE: And drool.

JOSHUA *(thinking):* Because I listen to you. You make my salivary glands ache.

MAUDE: You must be glad I'm here.

JOSHUA *(thinking):* Wrong.

MAUDE: Well, I'm glad to do it, Joshua. I am. I would . . . *(Begins to cry again)* I would want someone to do the same for me if I were a vegetable.

JOSHUA *(thinking):* A what?

MAUDE: It's so sad.

JOSHUA *(thinking):* Who're you callin' a "vegetable," you old prune?

MAUDE *(begins looking for a tissue):* Oh, now my nose is running. Where are my tissues? *(Can't find them)* Oh . . . what am I . . . ? *(Thinks of an idea, looks around, pulls at* JOSHUA*'s blanket.)*

JOSHUA *(thinking):* Hey. What do you think you're doing?

(She blows and wipes her nose on his blanket as he watches helplessly.)

JOSHUA *(thinking):* Stop that. Stop it. Oh . . . that's disgusting.

MAUDE: There. That's much better.

JOSHUA *(thinking):* For who? This used to be my favorite blanket.

(PASTOR JENNINGS *enters. He is fairly old too.)*

PASTOR: Well, well, well . . . here you are.

MAUDE: Oh! Hello, Pastor Jennings. How are you?

PASTOR: Just dandy. How are you, Maude?

MAUDE: My arthritis in my back is bothering me again. Would you lay hands on it?

PASTOR: Maybe later. How's Joshua?

MAUDE: The same. He'll probably die soon.

JOSHUA *(thinking):* You're a wonder, Maude.

PASTOR: You say that every time I come to visit.

MAUDE: He will.

PASTOR: We all will.

MAUDE: My eyes are getting weaker, too, Pastor. The doctor says I need new glasses. They're so heavy now they hurt my nose. Don't know what I'm gonna do. Will you lay hands on my eyes?

PASTOR: We'll see.

MAUDE: I need your prayers too. It's not easy, you know.

PASTOR: I know. And I think it's wonderful the way you take a personal interest in Joshua.

JOSHUA *(thinking):* Ha. She thinks she's going to get my Social Security when I die.

MAUDE: I think God wants us to be responsible for poor, miserable wretches.

JOSHUA *(thinking):* You're digging it deeper, Maude.

MAUDE: It's not easy.

PASTOR: I'm sure it isn't.

JOSHUA *(thinking):* I'm gonna hurt this woman. Just wait till she comes to help me with my bedpan again.

MAUDE: I do it with joy, though.

PASTOR: Good for you. The Lord will bless your kindness.

MAUDE: He better. I mean, He will. Well, I'll leave you to counsel him. He needs it—though he probably doesn't understand a word any of us are saying.

JOSHUA *(thinking):* That's where you're wrong, my dear. And I'm keeping track.

PASTOR: I'm sure deep inside he does.

MAUDE: It'd have to be *way* deep, Pastor. *Way* deep. Good-bye, Joshua.

JOSHUA *(thinking):* Bye, Maude. Don't hurry back.

MAUDE: No need to thank me.

JOSHUA *(thinking):* I wouldn't dream of it. You'll get the cleaning bill for my blanket.

MAUDE: Give us a kiss.

JOSHUA *(thinking):* No, anything but that.

(MAUDE *kisses him.)*

JOSHUA *(thinking):* Gross!

MAUDE: Bye.

(MAUDE *exits. After she has gone . . .)*

PASTOR: Maude means well.

JOSHUA *(thinking):* I know it. In another life, I would probably like her a lot.

(PASTOR *turns* JOSHUA *to face him and pulls up a chair.)*

PASTOR: Well, Josh—how'ya doin?

JOSHUA *(thinking):* Much better now, thanks. How are you, Frank?

PASTOR: Happy birthday, by the way.

JOSHUA *(thinking):* Thank you.

PASTOR: I was going to get you a card, but all I could find were the kind with funeral flowers and bad poetry.

JOSHUA *(thinking):* You're a good man.

PASTOR: I looked for a funny one, but they were all rather risque with pictures of voluptuous women. I didn't want to lead you into another stroke.

JOSHUA *(thinking):* It's the thought that counts.

PASTOR: I brought you a present, though. It's in your room.

JOSHUA *(thinking):* You didn't have to do that.

PASTOR: It's the entire Bible recorded on cassette. I know it's tough for you to read. Once a day I'll have the orderly play some of it for you. You can even have them fast forward through the genealogies.

JOSHUA *(thinking):* You're very thoughtful, Frank.

(PASTOR *looks at him a moment.)*

PASTOR: I wonder if Maude's right. I wonder if you really *don't* understand what I'm saying.

JOSHUA *(thinking):* I do, Frank. It's when you preached that I got confused.

PASTOR: Sometimes I wonder how you cope.

JOSHUA *(thinking):* Cope? Cope with what?

PASTOR: Is it faith? I hope so, but it's hard to understand. I've always taught that faith would get us through the *big* crises like marriage problems, financial struggles, church conflicts, family struggles . . . even death. But I was never sure how my faith would hold up against gray hair, or ears that don't hear like they used to, or strange spots on my skin or . . . *(pause)* not being able to take care of myself because my body has given up before the rest of me has.

JOSHUA *(thinking):* It used to bother me too.

PASTOR: The church is asking for my resignation, Josh.

JOSHUA *(thinking):* What?

PASTOR *(smiles):* I guess they didn't have the patience to wait for me to die.

JOSHUA *(thinking):* They can't do that!

PASTOR: They've been very kind about it. Nothing scandalous or overt—just some very subtle hints and quiet meetings. And then, there they were, standing in my living room, shuffling their feet, asking me to resign.

JOSHUA *(thinking):* It's outrageous!

PASTOR: At first I was hurt. But the more I thought about it, the more I see the sense of it.

JOSHUA *(thinking):* Sense? What sense?

PASTOR: A younger pastor with some new ideas is what they need.

JOSHUA *(thinking):* Ha! Where will a younger pastor get your wisdom and experience?

PASTOR: He'll need time to learn—to grow—but I did too. I can't think of a better church to do it in.

JOSHUA *(thinking):* Well, you've got me on that one.

PASTOR *(sighs):* I guess my biggest problem is . . . well, this is the first time I've had to think about being old. Can you believe it? I *am* old, I know, but I never had to *think* about it before.

JOSHUA *(thinking):* Funny—I've been thinking about it too.

PASTOR: I'm scared, Josh. I feel very . . . alone. I wish you could talk. I wish you could tell me it'll be all right.

JOSHUA *(thinking):* Don't let it worry you, Frank. It's kind of like the Lord is going through the house turning off the lights before we leave for vacation. He's doing it one room at a time—sometimes slower than I want. But I know we're leaving soon.

PASTOR *(pause):* I miss you, Josh.

*(*PASTOR *puts his head down in his hands. With great effort,* JOSHUA *reaches out to him and touches his shoulder.* PASTOR *looks up, surprised. They look at each other tenderly.* PASTOR *takes his hand and holds it with great affection.)*

PASTOR: Thanks, Josh.

(JOSHUA *relaxes.)*

PASTOR: Pray for me.

JOSHUA *(thinking):* I will, Frank. I *do.* The Lord isn't finished with either one of us.

(MAUDE *returns with a camera.)*

MAUDE: All right, I hope you're done talking. *(She giggles.)* Well, you know what I mean. I want to get a birthday picture of the two of you to hang up in Joshua's room—right next to mine. Though heaven knows we might not be here by the time it develops. But it's worth trying. Now, get over next to him, Pastor. Good. Do your best to smile, Joshua.

(With a bright flash, she takes the picture.)

(Black out)